Disease

Debbie Nevins

www.av2books.com

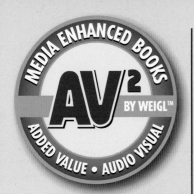

AV² provides enriched content that supplements and complements this book. Weigl's AV² books strive to create inspired learning and engage young minds in a total learning experience.

Your AV² Media Enhanced books come alive with...

Audio
Listen to sections of the book read aloud.

Key Words
Study vocabulary, and complete a matching word activity.

Video
Watch informative video clips.

Quizzes
Test your knowledge.

Embedded Weblinks
Gain additional information for research.

Slide Show
View images and captions, and prepare a presentation.

Try This!
Complete activities and hands-on experiments.

... and much, much more!

Go to **www.av2books.com,** and enter this book's unique code.

BOOK CODE

L603367

AV² by Weigl brings you media enhanced books that support active learning.

Download the AV² catalog at
www.av2books.com/catalog

AV² Online Navigation on page 48

Published by AV² by Weigl
350 5th Avenue, 59th Floor
New York, NY 10118

Websites: www.av2books.com   www.weigl.com

Copyright ©2015 AV² by Weigl

Library of Congress Control Number: 2014940092

ISBN 978-1-4896-1094-2 (hardcover)
ISBN 978-1-4896-1095-9 (softcover)
ISBN 978-1-4896-1096-6 (single-user eBook)
ISBN 978-1-4896-1097-3 (multi-user eBook)

Printed in the United States of America in North Mankato, Minnesota
1 2 3 4 5 6 7 8 9 0 18 17 16 15 14

052014
WEP090514

Weigl acknowledges Getty Images as its primary image supplier for this title.

Every reasonable effort has been made to trace ownership and to obtain permission to reprint copyright material. The publishers would be pleased to have any errors or omissions brought to their attention so that they may be corrected in subsequent printings.

Project Coordinator: Aaron Carr
Art Director: Terry Paulhus

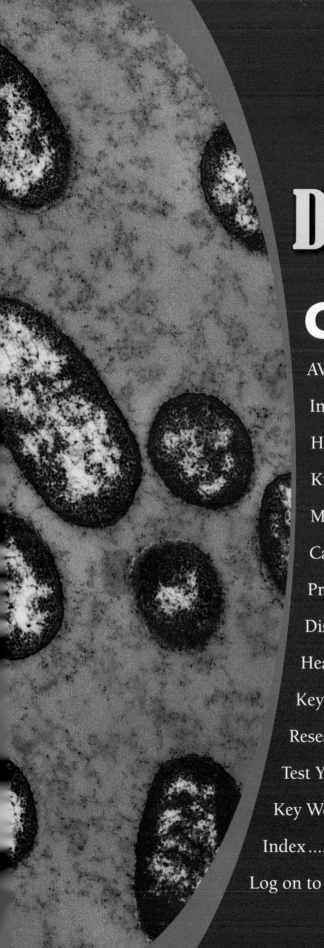

Disease

CONTENTS

Introduction to Disease

As long as there has been life on Earth, there have been diseases. Throughout history, people have developed many ways to treat illness and heal the sick. Some ways have been more effective than others. Today, medical advances help many people live longer, healthier lives than in the past. However, some diseases have not been overcome, and millions of people around the world do not have access to the best medical care.

History of Disease

"Human history has been changed by powerful germs too small to see."

Kinds of Diseases

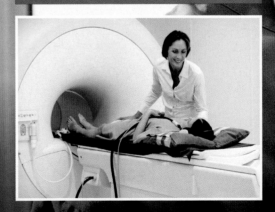

"Scientists classify diseases by their causes and symptoms."

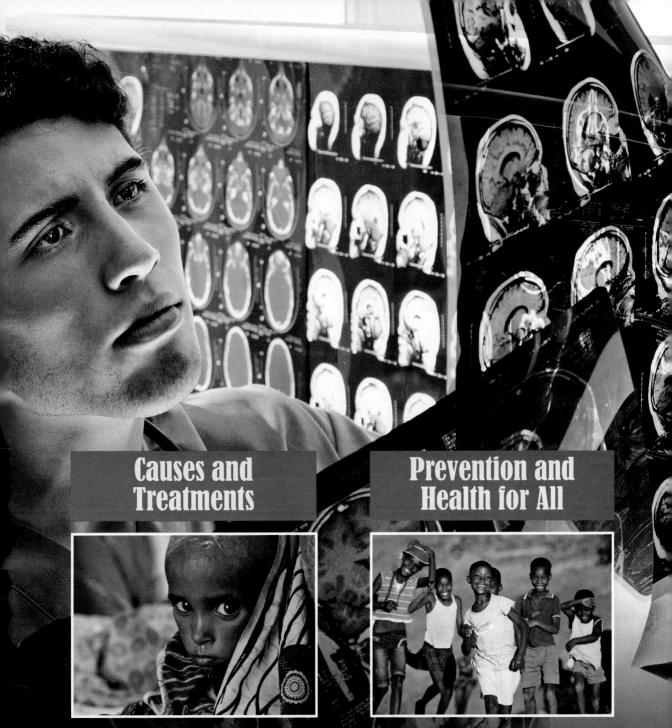

Causes and Treatments

"Various diseases can cause similar symptoms but require different kinds of care."

Prevention and Health for All

"Most doctors believe that trying to prevent illness is the best path to good health for all people.

History of Disease

KEY CONCEPTS

1 The Rise of Human Communities

2 Epidemics

3 Old Beliefs and Treatments

4 The Age of Modern Medicine

5 Developing Countries

istory is often told as the story of great people and events. However, human history has also been influenced by powerful forces that are too small to see. They are the **microbes** that cause disease. They are just as strong today as they were when humankind began.

1 The Rise of Human Communities

Many thousands of years ago, humans lived in small groups of hunters and gatherers. These people roamed the countryside in search of food. They had to cope with **infections** and other illnesses caused by **parasites**, which they often caught from the animals they hunted. Many people had worms, such as tapeworms, living in their digestive systems. Over the centuries, people found that certain plants had healing qualities. They used them to help treat illnesses.

With the development of agriculture, humans could have a more certain food supply by staying in one place, where they grew crops and raised livestock. People formed larger communities. They lived close to cattle, goats, pigs, and poultry.

Many common human diseases originally came from these animals. **Smallpox** and **tuberculosis** came from cattle. Measles came from dogs and cattle. Influenza, or flu, came from pigs, ducks, and chickens, and the common cold from horses.

Over time, large cities developed. As they grew, thousands of people lived alongside rodents and insects. This was an ideal environment for the spread of disease.

The rise and fall of civilizations were linked to diseases. When Europeans came to the Americas in large numbers in the 1500s, they brought smallpox, measles, flu, and other infections. The native peoples had never encountered these germs, and their bodies had no natural defenses against them. The diseases spread rapidly, killing about 90 percent of the people. In the European conquest of the Americas, disease was the most powerful weapon.

Spanish explorer Hernán Cortés's soldiers brought smallpox to Mexico.

2 Epidemics

When a disease spreads rapidly and affects a large number of people at the same time, the event is called an epidemic, or a plague. Outbreaks can spread across cities, countries, continents, or even the world. An especially far-reaching epidemic is called a pandemic. Most outbreaks eventually run their course and then end. Some epidemics have such major effects that they change the course of history.

Between 1346 and 1350, the Black Death killed 20 million people in Europe, or about one-third of the continent's population. People called this epidemic the Black Death because of the black spots the disease produced on the skin of its victims. However, no one knew what caused the illness. Terrified people blamed it on everything from the anger of God to bad air coming from swamps.

Today, most scientists believe the disease was bubonic plague. This disease is spread by fleas that have bitten infected rats and then bite humans. The Black Death had major effects on many aspects of European life. People in unaffected areas were afraid to travel. Trade between different parts of Europe declined, and wars were ended. Peasants who farmed for large landowners died in huge numbers. The landowners had to pay people to work their fields.

From 1918 to 1919, more people died of influenza than during the four years of the Black Death. The strain, or type, of influenza that caused the epidemic was called Spanish flu. The epidemic began while many nations were fighting in World War I. The fact that millions of soldiers were living in crowded and unsanitary conditions helped the outbreak spread quickly. Flu was not new, but the 1918–1919 strain was especially dangerous. It infected about one-fifth of the world's population and killed 25 million people. In the United States, the death toll was about 675,000. That was more than ten times the number of Americans killed in battle during World War I.

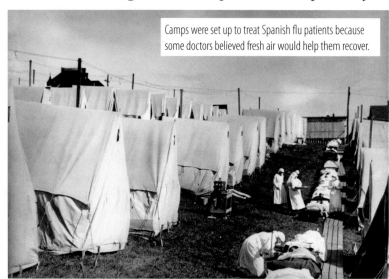
Camps were set up to treat Spanish flu patients because some doctors believed fresh air would help them recover.

Is HIV/AIDS Still a Crisis?

First identified in 1981, the disease Acquired Immune Deficiency Syndrome (AIDS) rapidly expanded into a deadly epidemic. Since the epidemic began, nearly 30 million people with AIDS have died worldwide. In the epidemic's early years, very little was understood about the disease. Eventually, scientists made the connection between HIV, a virus, and AIDS, the disease it causes. They developed new medicines, and people also learned about ways to prevent the disease from spreading. At least in the world's wealthier countries, many infected people are now living with, rather than dying of, HIV/AIDS. Illness is also spreading more slowly in many areas.

International AIDS Organizations

In 2012, HIV/AIDS killed 1.6 million people, many of them in Africa. The disease is still a crisis, especially in regions where many people are poor and do not have access to good health care. It is important to continue researching better medications and helping those who have become ill.

Some Health Professionals

Even in areas where fewer people are dying of AIDs or becoming infected with HIV, it is still important to take this disease very seriously. Once a person has HIV, he or she is infected for life. At present, there is no cure. AIDS is a heavy burden to manage for a lifetime.

Some Medical Researchers

There is no question that AIDS is a serious disease, and efforts to prevent, treat, and cure it should continue. However, there is a limited amount of money available for medical research. Fighting other major illnesses, such as cancer and heart disease, also needs to be supported.

HIV/AIDS Deniers

Today, AIDS is not a big risk anymore. With the current medicines, it is easy to control. Some people try to make the problem seem more serious than it really is.

| For | Supportive | Undecided | Unsupportive | Against |

3 Old Beliefs and Treatments

The ways that people have regarded disease and healing have changed greatly over the centuries. Some aspects of modern medicine can be traced to ancient times. The Hippocratic Oath, a doctor's promise of good medical conduct, was written in the fifth century BC in Greece. A modern version of it is still in use today.

Other beliefs that endured for thousands of years have been discarded. From ancient Greece through the 18th century, Western medicine was based on the theory of the humors. The human body was thought to contain four fluids, or humors. They were black bile, yellow bile, blood, and phlegm. Each person had a special combination of these fluids, which accounted for his or her overall nature. Good health depended on keeping the humors in balance. When they were out of balance, the person became ill.

A common remedy was the practice of bloodletting. An ill person might be diagnosed as suffering from an excess of blood. A surgeon, who was often also a barber and a dentist, would cut a vein in the patient's arm, leg, or neck. The blood would flow into a measuring cup.

Other common practices for dealing with a medical problem in one part of the body included cupping and applying leeches. In cupping, hot glass cups were placed on the skin to create sores that would bleed. Leeches are blood-sucking worms that were put on the skin. Today, most of these beliefs and practices have been proved wrong and not effective. However, some old practices are still used as treatments, especially in **alternative medicine**. For example, cupping is used to massage muscles and reduce pain.

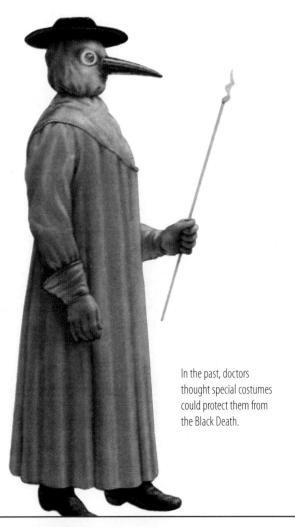

In the past, doctors thought special costumes could protect them from the Black Death.

4 The Age of Modern Medicine

In past centuries, the ability of physicians, or doctors, to understand disease was limited by what they could not see. They could not see the smallest structures inside the human body. They could not see microbes and did not know they existed.

Scientists first began building **microscopes** in the 16th century. In the late 17th century, Dutch inventor Antony van Leeuwenhoek created microscopes powerful enough to see tiny structures and forms of life. He discovered blood **cells** and several types of microbes, including bacteria. However, the role these microbes played in disease was not understood at first.

In the 19th century, French scientist Louis Pasteur began exploring their roles. His experiments revealed that germs are passed from one living thing to another. At the time, scientists had thought that bacteria appeared on their own, out of nowhere. Pasteur also invented a process, that became known as pasteurization. It kills harmful bacteria in milk by using heat. His research improved scientists' understanding of the concept of immunization. This is the idea that, with the help of a vaccine, a person can develop natural protection against an illness caused by a microbe. A vaccine contains a tiny amount of that microbe. Immunization has become widely used and very important in preventing disease.

Pasteur's discoveries suggested a link between sanitation and health. In the 19th century, surgeons often did not wash their hands before performing an operation. They did not realize that germs on their hands could infect the patient. It would take decades for doctors to realize the importance of performing surgery in an antiseptic, or germ-free, environment. Understanding the connection between germs, sanitation, and disease led to major changes in medical science.

Louis Pasteur developed a vaccine against rabies, a disease that some animals can pass to humans.

5 Developing Countries

The 20th century saw rapid advances in the treatment of illnesses. Diseases such as **polio**, tuberculosis, and **diphtheria** once caused the deaths of many people in all parts of the world. These sicknesses were largely eliminated in the United States and other **developed countries**.

The situation is different in many **developing countries**. Poor people living in these countries often do not have access to healthful food and clean water. Developing countries may not have enough modern hospitals, doctors, and other trained health-care workers. Medicines may be in short supply or too costly for many people. Poor transportation systems make it especially hard for people in the countryside to get medical care. Many diseases that are now rare or easy to treat in developed nations are still common and often deadly in developing countries.

Other factors also affect people's health in developing nations. Governments may not have or want to use money for health-care programs. Some countries do not have or do not enforce laws against pollution that can damage the air and water, causing health problems.

Developing countries with poor health-care systems are also often not prepared to deal with the effects of a natural disaster. Haiti, for example, is one of the poorest countries on Earth. In October 2010, an earthquake there killed more than 200,000 people. Many other people were injured, and more than 1 million were left homeless and without clean water. **Cholera** broke out and quickly became an epidemic. As of late 2013, more than 684,000 cases and 8,000 deaths had been reported.

Leading Causes of Death in Low-Income Countries

(number of deaths per 100,000 people in 2011)

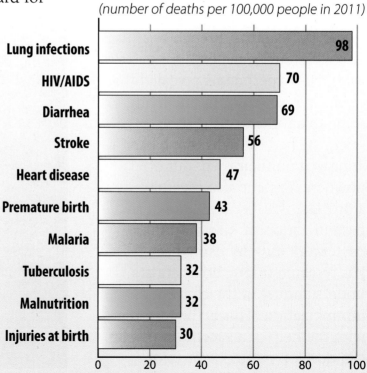

Cause	Deaths per 100,000
Lung infections	98
HIV/AIDS	70
Diarrhea	69
Stroke	56
Heart disease	47
Premature birth	43
Malaria	38
Tuberculosis	32
Malnutrition	32
Injuries at birth	30

Is Health Care a Human Right?

In 1948, the United Nations (UN) Universal Declaration of Human Rights stated, "Everyone has the right to a standard of living adequate for the health and well-being of himself and of his family, including . . . medical care." However, by the early 21st century, the UN's goal had not been achieved. In 2012, 1.3 billion people around the world had no access to health care.

Human Rights Organizations	**Some Health-Care Professionals**	**Some Health-Care Economists**	**Conservative Political Leaders**
Everyone has the right to good health care. When people are healthy, they lead better and longer lives. In addition, they are able to use their ideas and their labor to make society better for everyone. The world benefits when health care is available to all.	Good health care for every person may not be possible to achieve. However, governments must give priority to programs that improve people's health. This includes programs to build hospitals, train doctors, control pollution, provide clean water, and educate people about good health practices.	Health care is a worthwhile goal. However, it is costly to achieve, and governments have limited funds. Money spent on health care cannot be spent on other important goals, such as building schools. The benefits of health-care programs must be balanced against their costs.	Health care costs money. When governments use a great deal of money for health-care programs, taxes have to be raised to pay for them. It is not fair to give some people a right by placing a burden on other people.

For   Supportive   Undecided   Unsupportive   Against

Kinds of Diseases

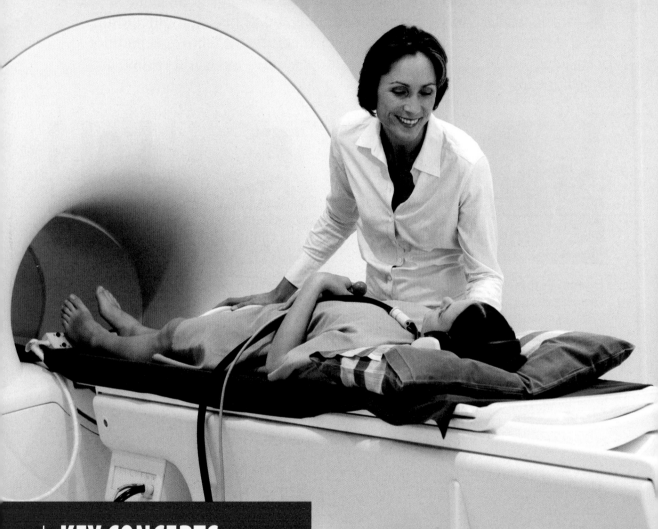

D

iseases come in many forms. Scientists classify diseases by their causes and symptoms. They also look at whether a disease can be passed from one person to another and how long it lasts.

1 Infectious Diseases

Microbes, which are also called microorganisms, live almost everywhere. Most are harmless. Some, however, cause diseases. Certain types of bacteria, viruses, and fungi can make people ill.

Any illness that can pass from one living thing to another is called an infectious disease. *Contagious* and *communicable* are other terms that mean the same thing as infectious. Examples of infectious diseases range from the common cold to HIV/AIDS. Although different infections are passed on in various ways, all contagious diseases spread when people come in contact with the germs that cause them.

Infections can spread through the air or through direct contact. Sneezing and coughing can send tiny droplets of a sick person's **mucus** and saliva into the air. The fluids, which contain germs, may land on other people. Those people then spread the germs to their own eyes, noses, or mouths.

People can pick up germs by touching or swallowing food or water that contains microbes. Sometimes, people can catch germs from touching infected animals, from bites or scratches, or from handling animal waste. Insects are common disease carriers. Mosquitoes, fleas, lice, or ticks can transfer germs from an animal to a human.

Most infectious diseases are acute, or short-term, illnesses. A cold, for example, usually goes away in one or two weeks. However, acute diseases can be deadly. Infectious diseases cause about one-third of deaths worldwide each year. Of those, six diseases result in 90 percent of the deaths. They are **pneumonia**, diseases that cause diarrhea, tuberculosis, malaria, measles, and HIV/AIDs.

Germs in droplets of mucus and saliva can live on surfaces, such as doorknobs, for up to two hours.

2 Noncommunicable Diseases

A noncommunicable disease, or NCD, is a one that is not infectious. It cannot be passed from one person to another. Diseases of the circulatory system, including heart disease and high blood pressure, are common serious NCDs. Other examples of NCDs include cancer, **diabetes**, **Alzheimer's disease**, and respiratory, or lung, diseases.

These diseases often develop as people age. Some NCDs are caused by being exposed to certain substances at work or in the environment. NCDs may also arise from lifestyle choices. For example, smoking puts people at high risk for lung cancer, several other types of cancer, and other lung diseases. Diets that are very high in fat or that cause a person to become obese, or severely overweight, can lead to illnesses such as diabetes, heart disease, and stroke. A stroke occurs when a blood vessel in the brain breaks or becomes blocked.

NCDs are often chronic, or long-term, medical conditions that progress slowly. The harmful effects of cigarette smoke, chemicals in the environment, or a high-fat diet may take years to become serious. Many chronic diseases also require long-term treatment. This may include taking certain medications for the rest of a patient's life.

Chronic NCDs are, by far, the leading cause of death around the world. More than 36 million people die every year from NCDs. That is nearly two-thirds of total deaths that occur worldwide.

Leading Causes of Death in High-Income Countries

(number of deaths per 100,000 people in 2011)

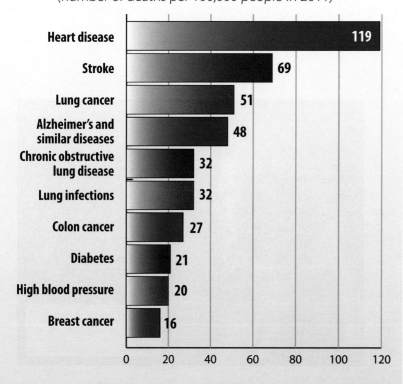

Cause	Deaths
Heart disease	119
Stroke	69
Lung cancer	51
Alzheimer's and similar diseases	48
Chronic obstructive lung disease	32
Lung infections	32
Colon cancer	27
Diabetes	21
High blood pressure	20
Breast cancer	16

Should the U.S. Government Support Embryonic Stem Cell Research?

An embryo forms after an egg is **fertilized**. Some embryos are grown in vitro, or in a laboratory, when a woman has trouble becoming pregnant. Many of these embryos are never used. In 1998, scientists learned how to remove stem cells from such embryos. Embryonic stem cells can grow into any kind of human cell. Scientists hope they can be used in sick people to replace cells that have been destroyed by disease. However, some people object to medical research using embryonic stem cells.

People with Incurable Diseases

This research can saves lives, and the federal government should be paying for it. The cells scientists study come from embryos that will not be used for any other purpose anyway.

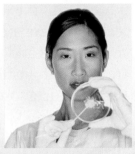

Some Medical Researchers

Stem cell research is important. The government should help pay for it, but there must be strict rules about the ways that government money can be used. These rules will make sure research is conducted properly.

Some Doctors

Using embryonic stem cells may not be necessary. Scientists studying stem cells taken from adults have already made progress. Priority can be given to research that does not use cells taken from embryos.

Some Religious Groups

Embryonic stem cell research should never be done. We believe an embryo is a form of human life. It is wrong to take a human life, even for medical research that might save the lives of sick people.

| For | Supportive | Undecided | Unsupportive | Against |

3 Cancer

Cancer is the term for a group of diseases affecting cells in different parts of the body. The human body has many types of cells. Each type carries out specific functions to keep the body alive and healthy. Normally, cells divide and produce replacements as old or damaged cells die. Cancer occurs when this process goes wrong. Some cells mutate, or change, to an abnormal form. The abnormal cells then divide and grow very quickly. Often, a mass of abnormal cells called a tumor develops. Over time, the abnormal cells usually invade other body parts, and more tumors grow.

There are more than 100 different types of cancer. Most are named for the **organ** in which they start. For example, cancer that begins in the stomach is called stomach cancer.

Not many decades ago, people who developed cancer were very likely to die from the disease. Cancer is still a serious illness and a leading cause of death. However, today many cancer patients are able to survive the disease. There are more than 11 million cancer survivors in the United States.

One reason for improved survival is early detection. Most cancers are easier to treat if they are diagnosed, or found, soon after they develop. There are now screening tests for many types of cancer. These are medical tests that allow doctors to find cancer before the disease advances to the point that the patient feels ill. There are also many new medications and other forms of treatment to fight cancer once it has been diagnosed.

People can reduce their risk of ever getting some types of cancer by taking certain steps. Using sunscreen helps protect against skin cancer. Not drinking large amounts of alcohol lowers one's chances of developing liver cancer.

Medical devices that take pictures of the brain can show the presence of a tumor.

4 Genetic and Childhood Diseases

Children can develop some types of noncommunicable diseases. Sometimes, they are born with them. Some illnesses common in children are the result of a combination of factors, such as environment and family history. Asthma, which causes breathing problems, may be one of these illnesses. Conditions before birth also play a role. For example, if a pregnant woman drinks alcohol or smokes cigarettes, her unborn child is at risk of developing health problems.

Some children are born with genetic diseases. These result from abnormalities in specific genes. Genes are tiny units within a cell that determine the characteristics of an organism, such as eye and hair color.

They are the set of instructions encoded inside each human cell that tell the cell what functions to perform. This information is inherited from one's parents. Humans have about 23,000 genes. Sometimes, there is a mistake in the genetic information. For example, in the disease sickle-cell anemia, a genetic defect causes red blood cells to have an irregular shape. This makes it hard for them to travel normally through the body.

Some genetic disorders, such as **Down syndrome**, are evident at birth. Others, including the lung disease cystic fibrosis, become apparent in infancy or childhood. Still other genetic disorders, such as Huntington's disease, a brain disorder, may not show up until adulthood.

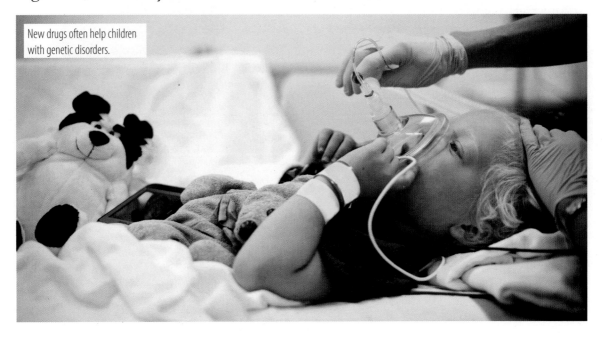

New drugs often help children with genetic disorders.

Mapping Life Expectancy

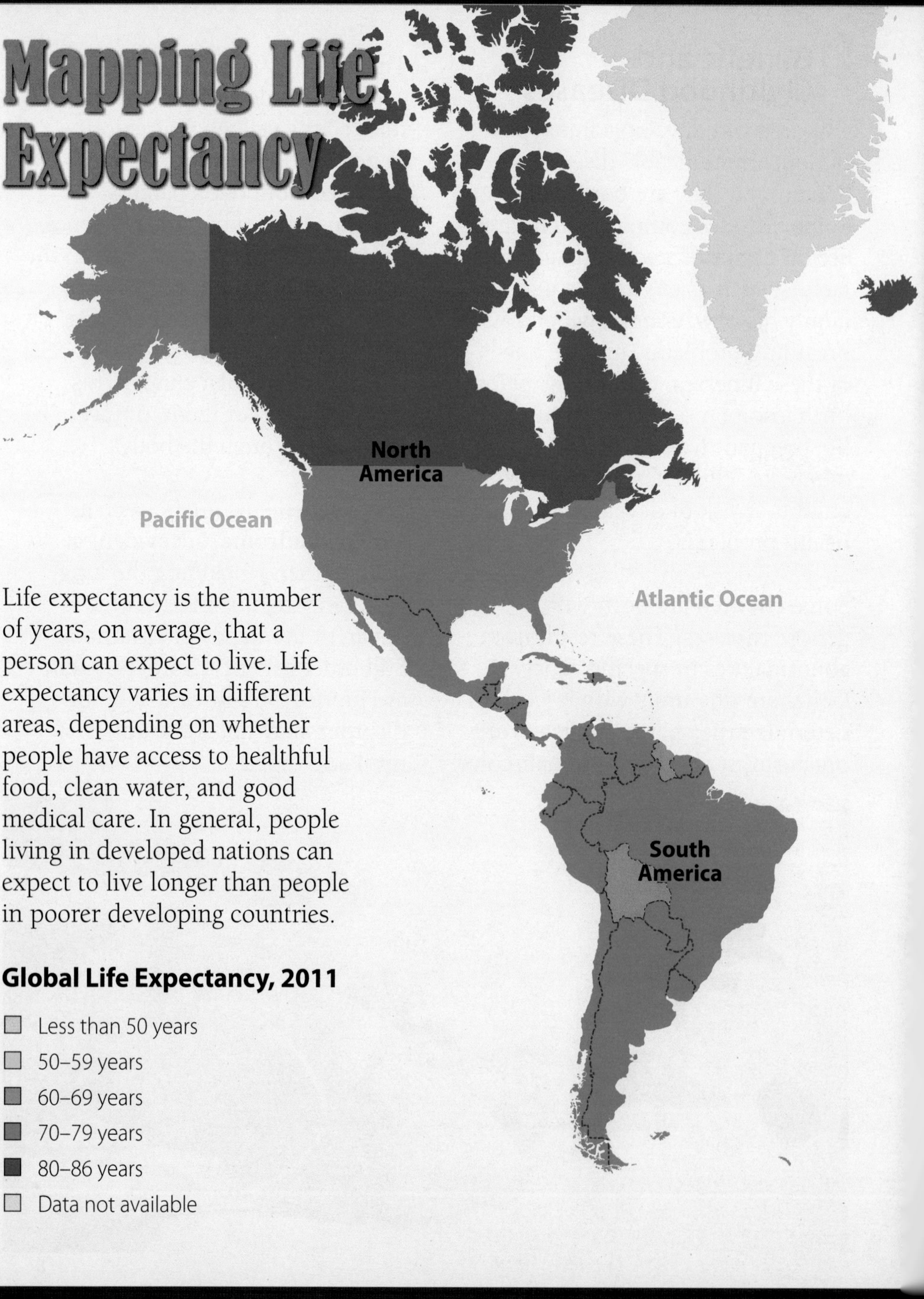

North America

Pacific Ocean

Atlantic Ocean

Life expectancy is the number of years, on average, that a person can expect to live. Life expectancy varies in different areas, depending on whether people have access to healthful food, clean water, and good medical care. In general, people living in developed nations can expect to live longer than people in poorer developing countries.

South America

Global Life Expectancy, 2011

- ☐ Less than 50 years
- ☐ 50–59 years
- ☐ 60–69 years
- ☐ 70–79 years
- ☐ 80–86 years
- ☐ Data not available

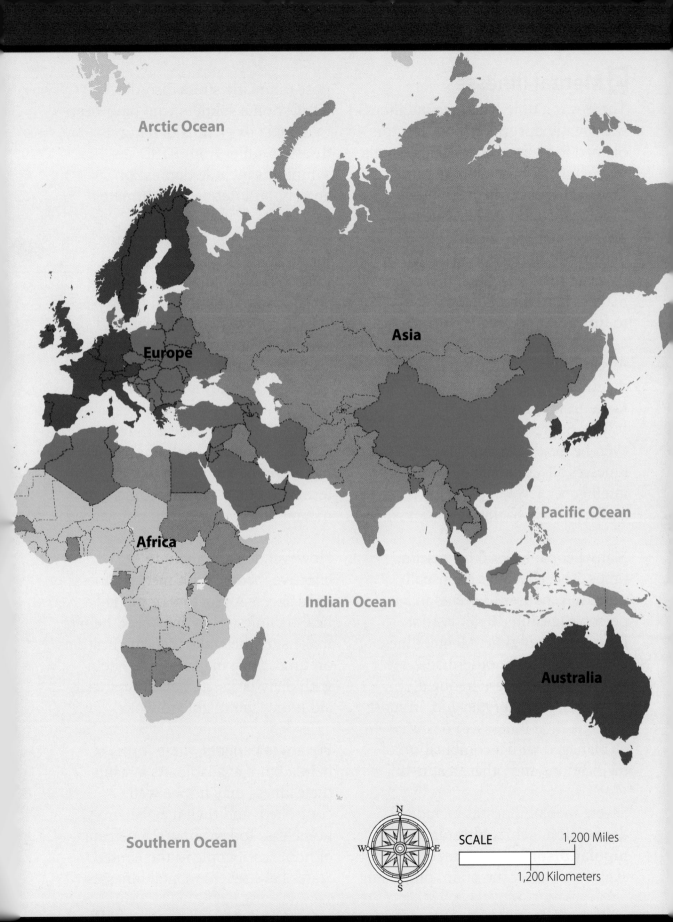

Arctic Ocean

Asia

Europe

Pacific Ocean

Africa

Indian Ocean

Australia

Southern Ocean

SCALE

1,200 Miles

1,200 Kilometers

N
W   E
S

5 Mental Illnesses

There was a time when mental illness was greatly misunderstood. Doctors blamed it on poor character, demons, witchcraft, or other supernatural forces. However, mental illness is a medical condition just like any physical ailment. It disrupts a person's thinking, moods, and ability to relate to others. Such illness can make it hard for a person to function in daily life.

As with physical diseases, mental illnesses can range from mild to severe. Some can even be deadly. Mental illnesses affect people of every intelligence level, race, culture, and economic background.

"Mental illness affects people of every race, culture, and economic background."

Many people feel sad or upset at times. Those feelings are usually normal responses to events in a person's life and do not last for long periods of time. Mental illness symptoms, on the other hand, are ongoing. They cause frequent disruptions in everyday life. In most cases, mental illness can be cured or managed with a combination of medications and other treatment.

Severe mental illnesses include **depression**, **schizophrenia**, and **bipolar disorder**. Extremely stressful events can affect the brain, producing post-traumatic stress disorder, or PTSD. Some soldiers who have been in combat or victims of natural disasters suffer from PTSD. Its symptoms include depression, anxiety, and frequent nightmares.

Until the 1960s, it was common for mentally ill people to be put in special hospitals for life. Living conditions in these places were often poor, and sick people were commonly mistreated. As those conditions became known, many hospitals were closed. In recent years, with improved medications, long-term or even short-term hospital stays for people with mental illnesses are often not needed.

However, for treatment to be effective, people with mental illnesses need access to doctors or mental health clinics. They may need help to make sure they take their medications on time. They may also need help with daily tasks, as well as financial aid if they are unable to work.

For some patients, these forms of help are not available. As a result, their illness may not be well controlled, and they may become homeless. Today, about 26 percent of homeless people in the United States have severe mental illnesses.

Should Mentally Ill People Be Forced to Accept Treatment?

With certain illnesses, such as schizophrenia, the sick person may refuse to see a doctor or take medication. Schizophrenia affects more than 2 million Americans. Of those, some 40 percent are unable to understand that they have the disorder. Most mentally ill people are not violent. Still, there are times when they are in danger of hurting themselves or others. For this reason, family members, doctors, and governments may consider involuntary treatment to be necessary.

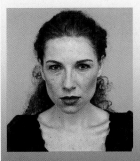

Advocates of Involuntary Treatment

Some 3.6 million American adults with severe mental illness do not receive treatment each year. They are at risk for suicide and abuse by other people. Some could be violent. It is best to force these people to get the help they need.

State Government Leaders

The state must protect all its citizens. State laws have to protect the rights of sick people. However, in cases where mental illness puts a person at risk of self-harm or makes the person a threat to others, we should be able to require treatment.

Disability Rights Organizations

Involuntary treatment can be unfair to people with mental illness. Doctors or government officials do not take action against people who fail to take their heart medications. People with mental illness should not be treated differently.

Some Former Patients

Being put in a mental hospital without a choice is often a frightening and damaging experience. It can make sick people worse. Any type of forced treatment violates people's rights.

For   Supportive   Undecided   Unsupportive   Against

Causes and Treatments

KEY CONCEPTS

Doctors often try to do more than just treat a person's symptoms, such as a cough or ache. They try to determine what is causing the illness. Then, they use treatments that they think will cure the disease. Various diseases can cause similar symptoms but require different kinds of care.

1 Parasites and Tropical Diseases

Human beings have up to 100 trillion other organisms living on or in their bodies. Most of these parasites are microbes, and each person has about 5 pounds (2.3 kilograms) of them. They live in a person's mouth, in the intestines, on the skin, and in many other parts of the body.

Some parasites that live on or in humans are large enough to be visible to the eye. Worms can grow in people's digestive systems, blood vessels, and other organs. Tapeworms in the intestines can develop to 20 feet (6 meters) long.

People can get parasites by eating food or drinking water that contains them. Microbes and visible parasites can cause a number of serious infectious diseases, including malaria and cholera. Some of these diseases are not easy to treat. Others are easily prevented or treated if good sanitation and medical care are available. However, they are major problems among poor people in developing nations. One billion people are affected by parasitic diseases worldwide. Most of these infections occur in tropical, or warm-climate, parts of the world. Such illnesses are sometimes called neglected tropical diseases (NTDs).

NTDs, which have been almost eliminated in developed nations, can be deadly. Intestinal worms kill 60,000 people each year, mainly children. Nonfatal parasitic diseases, such as **elephantiasis**, can also cause great suffering. They can leave their victims unable to work or attend school.

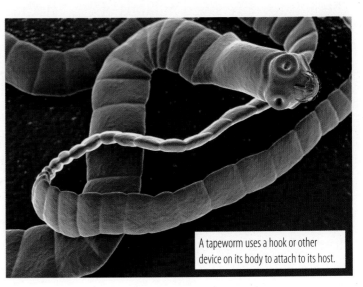

A tapeworm uses a hook or other device on its body to attach to its host.

2 Bacteria

Most kinds of bacteria are harmless to humans, and some are even helpful. Certain types are used to produce yogurt and cheese. Some forms of bacteria live in the body and help to digest food. Less than 1 percent of all types of bacteria cause diseases in humans. These disease-causing germs are responsible for illnesses such as **strep throat**, tuberculosis, some types of pneumonia, food poisoning, and certain skin infections.

To treat illnesses caused by bacteria, doctors often use antibiotics. They are a group of medicines that either kill bacteria or keep them from growing. The first antibiotic, penicillin, was discovered in 1928 and made into a usable medicine in 1941.

Since the 1940s, many types of antibiotics have been developed. These drugs have saved millions of lives and remain important forms of treatment. People taking antibiotics often recover from illnesses that can be deadly if not treated. By the 1970s, some common infectious diseases, such as tuberculosis, were close to vanishing because patients given antibiotics were not spreading germs.

However, doctors began to notice that some diseases were no longer

Scientists grow disease-causing bacteria in laboratories in order to study these microbes.

responding to the drugs that once cured them. Scientists concluded that bacteria exposed to antibiotics but not killed by them are able to mutate. These bacteria grow in new forms, sometimes called superbugs, which are capable of resisting antibiotics.

This discovery led many doctors to reduce their patients' use of antibiotics. Doctors now try to be careful to give patients these drugs only in cases where they are clearly necessary. By using antibiotics less, doctors hope to slow the development of superbug mutations.

Should People Use Antibacterial Cleaning Products?

Antibacterial soaps, hand cleansers, dishwashing liquids, and other cleaning products claim to kill germs that cause illness. The bacteria-killing ingredient in many of these products is Triclosan. It has been used for more than 40 years. However, some people think antibacterial products may cause more harm than good. These people are concerned that the wide use of antibacterial products may be contributing to the growth of superbugs.

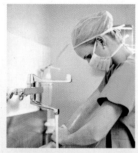

Soap Industry Executives

Antibacterial cleaning products are completely safe and effective. Triclosan has been tested for safety many times. There is no reason to believe it causes superbugs.

Government Health Officials

By killing bacteria on hands and kitchen items, antibacterial soaps can prevent illness. Unless future research shows that these products lead to a major increase in drug-resistant bacteria, they should continue to be used.

Some Scientists

There is evidence that soap with Triclosan is no more effective than washing with ordinary soap and water. It is certainly important to keep hands and kitchen utensils clean. However, if people just use regular soap carefully, there is no need for products with Triclosan.

Environmental Organizations

Chemicals such as Triclosan are just not safe. They may produce chemical changes in the body. They cause superbugs to develop. In addition, they build up in the soil, where crops are grown, and in sources of drinking water.

For   Supportive   Undecided   Unsupportive   Against

3 Viruses

About 1,000 times smaller than bacteria, viruses cause many types of illnesses. These microbes are too small to be seen with an ordinary microscope. Scientists can observe them only with a more powerful device called an electron microscope.

Viruses cannot function on their own. The only thing that they can do is replicate, or make copies of themselves. They can do that only when they are inside another cell, called a host cell. Once inside a human host cell, viruses rapidly make more viruses, which spread quickly to other cells in the body. The viruses destroy those cells, and the person gets sick.

Different viruses cause different infections. About 5,000 viruses have been studied in detail, but scientists know there are millions of types. Viruses cause colds, flu, chicken pox, polio, and other diseases.

Viruses can be passed from one person to another through direct contact, the transfer of body fluids, coughing, or sneezing. Antibiotics have no effect on viruses. However, the human body has some natural defenses against a viral attack. The body's immune system can produce cells called antibodies. These may prevent viruses from replicating or kill cells infected by a virus. Sometimes, the immune system raises the body's temperature, since heat slows down a virus's ability to replicate. This is why a person with a viral infection may have a fever.

Some viral diseases can be deadly. However, many viral infections simply run their course and disappear, such as a cold or a case of the flu. Some diseases, such as smallpox, can be protected against through vaccinations. In recent years, a number of drugs have been developed for specific viral diseases. Many of these drugs work by interfering with a virus's ability to replicate. Often, the drugs, such as HIV medications, cannot remove the virus from the body and cure the patient. However, they can keep the disease under control.

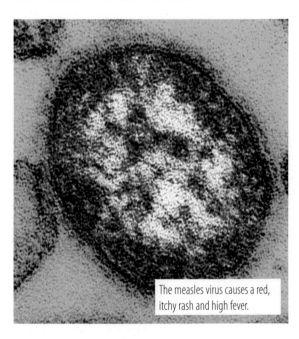

The measles virus causes a red, itchy rash and high fever.

4 Environmental and Lifestyle Diseases

Germs do not cause most chronic illnesses, especially in developed nations. Pollutants put into the environment and unhealthy lifestyle choices often help cause chronic diseases. These illnesses include cancer, heart disease, and stroke.

Heart disease is the number-one cause of death in the United States. Nearly 800,000 Americans die from heart disease each year. That figure represents nearly 30 percent of all U.S. deaths. In many people, a diet high in fat causes a substance called plaque to build up inside arteries over time. This can lead to blood clots and a lack of blood reaching the heart muscles or the brain. The result may be a heart attack or stroke. Lack of exercise, smoking, and drinking too much alcohol may also cause heart disease.

In the United States, two-thirds of adults and one-third of children are overweight. During the past 30 years, obesity has more than doubled in children and tripled in teenagers. An unhealthy diet and lack of exercise are two main causes of obesity. Obese people are more likely to develop diabetes, heart disease, certain kinds of cancer, and other serious health problems.

The greatest preventable cause of death in the world is cigarette smoking. Tobacco smoke contains more than 7,000 chemicals. Hundreds of these are toxic, or poisonous. At least 69 are known to cause cancer. Worldwide, tobacco use causes more than 5 million deaths per year. As the world's population increases, experts predict tobacco use will cause more than 8 million deaths annually by 2030, unless more people choose to not smoke.

Countries with the Most Smokers

Nearly two-thirds of the world's tobacco smokers live in 10 countries.

Percent of the world's smokers: 30%, 25%, 20%, 15%, 10%, 5%, 0%

China, India, Indonesia, Russia, United States, Japan, Brazil, Bangladesh, Germany, Turkey

Traditional Chinese medicine relies on ingredients from plants, animals, and minerals.

5 Non-Western and Alternative Medicine

As people fight disease, some turn to different sorts of medical therapies. Conventional, or Western, medicine is the main approach in North America, Europe, and developed nations in other regions. In Western medicine, a doctor examines the patient, diagnoses the illness, and then prescribes medication or another treatment, such as surgery, to cure that disease.

Other sorts of health care take a different approach. **Homeopathy** and **naturopathy** are just two of many alternative therapies. Ancient healing systems, such as traditional Chinese medicine, have been practiced for thousands of years. Some have become more widely used in recent years. Nearly 40 percent of U.S. adults report using alternative therapies in addition to, or in place of, conventional medicine.

Traditional Chinese medicine, for example, does not focus on a disease. It looks at a person's whole body, mind, and environment. It is based on the concept of an invisible energy called qi. This life force circulates in the body. If the flow of qi is blocked, illness results. Health is an ongoing process of restoring and maintaining balance and harmony in this flow.

A practitioner of traditional Chinese medicine often uses herbs, **acupuncture**, massage, and other techniques to produce well-being. Of these therapies, scientists have found the most evidence for the effectiveness of acupuncture. Western medicine is slowly adopting that practice, along with certain relaxation techniques used in alternative medicine.

Should Smoking Be Illegal in the United States?

Each year, there are more than 400,000 smoking-related deaths in the United States. Medical treatment of tobacco-related diseases costs almost $100 billion annually. Those costs result in higher health insurance rates for everyone. Some costs are paid by government health programs. Therefore, they may result in higher taxes or less money for other government activities. Some people think that lives and money could be saved by outlawing smoking.

Public Health Officials
If no one smoked in the United States, more than 1,000 lives would be saved every day. Strong action must be taken to prevent these needless deaths.

Many Americans
Before smoking is made illegal, we should be sure we have tried all other ways to reduce it as much as possible. Taxes on cigarettes can be increased to make them too expensive for many people. More advertising campaigns can be used to make sure people know the risks.

Some Political Leaders
I want to save lives and money, but making smoking illegal will very likely not work. In the early 1900s, the U.S. government made alcohol illegal. People did not stop drinking. Instead, crime increased, and gangs of criminals became rich by making and selling many types of alcoholic drinks.

Tobacco industry Executives
We sell our products to adults. They should be able to decide for themselves whether to buy cigarettes or not. Making cigarettes also provides jobs for thousands of people. They will all be out of work if smoking becomes illegal.

For   Supportive   Undecided   Unsupportive   Against

Prevention and Health for All

KEY CONCEPTS

1 Immunization

2 Access, Education, and Sanitation

3 Medical Advances and Life Expectancy

O ver time, scientists hope to find a cure for every disease. However, most doctors believe that trying to prevent illness as much as possible is the best path to good health for all people.

1 Immunization

In the United States and other developed nations, most infants and children are vaccinated against many infectious diseases. These include polio, tetanus, measles, mumps, and whooping cough. Teenagers and adults are advised to get flu shots and other vaccinations.

Widespread immunization has gone a long way toward eliminating many deadly diseases. For example, only about 100 to 200 cases of measles now occur in the United States each year. In 1920, almost 470,000 children and adults had measles, and more than 7,500 people died.

> "Immunization has gone a long way toward eliminating many diseases."

Smallpox can be a deadly disease. Many patients who survived the illness were left with scars. The first smallpox vaccine was developed in 1796. By the 1900s, immunization became widespread. In 1967, the World Health Organization (WHO) began a worldwide campaign to wipe out smallpox by making vaccination available to everyone. The campaign was successful. By 1979, smallpox had been eliminated.

2 Access, Education, and Sanitation

Many cases of noncommunicable diseases can also be prevented. In developed nations, an important part of prevention is education. Government and other programs try to convince people to adopt a lifestyle that promotes good health. Governments in many developed countries also have programs to make sure people have access to health care. If people see doctors regularly, illnesses are often diagnosed earlier.

Many people in developing nations face additional problems. In these countries, widespread poverty may mean that children suffer from malnutrition. Adults and even children may do hard physical labor in unsafe and unhealthy conditions. Many people do not have access to medical care, and children often do not receive immunizations. WHO, other international organizations, and many governments are working to improve living conditions and health care in the developing world.

3 Medical Advances and Life Expectancy

Conditions vary from country to country. Worldwide, however, more people live longer lives and enjoy better health today than ever before. With new equipment, doctors can find and begin to treat many diseases in their early stages. New drugs and other forms of treatment are more effective in curing or controlling disease than treatment techniques used in the past. A few decades ago, people diagnosed with many types of heart disease or with AIDS often could not expect to live much longer. That is no longer the case.

In 1955, the average life expectancy for the world's population was 48 years. By 2013, it had increased to 68 years. In the European country of Monaco, the average life expectancy is 84 years. This is the highest figure for any nation in the world. Many countries with the lowest life expectancies are developing nations in Central and Southern Africa. In countries such as Chad, Angola, and South Africa, people live, on average, to only about 50 years old. Although national and international programs to improve health in developing countries have made great progress, there is still a long way to go.

Deaths among Children under the Age of Five, by Region

In 2012, about 6.6 million children worldwide died before reaching the age of five. The portions of these deaths that occurred in different areas of the world varied a great deal. The highest percentages of total deaths were in regions with many developing countries.

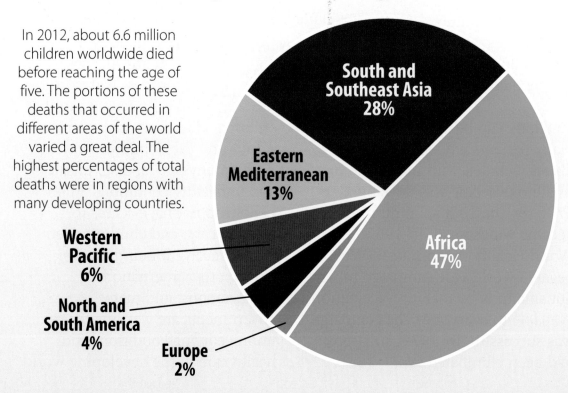

South and Southeast Asia 28%

Eastern Mediterranean 13%

Africa 47%

Western Pacific 6%

North and South America 4%

Europe 2%

Should All Children Be Required to Get Vaccinations?

The U.S. Centers for Disease Control and Prevention, as well as other health organizations, recommend that children be vaccinated against 15 common childhood illnesses. All 50 U.S. states require children to be vaccinated against certain illnesses before they can start school. Some parents, however, do not want to have their children vaccinated. They worry that vaccines may make their children ill or even lead to the development of conditions such as **autism**. In some cases, people oppose vaccination because of their religious beliefs.

State Government Officials
Children must be vaccinated before starting school, where so many young people are together in one place. A sick child can quickly infect many other children with a serious illness. The government has the authority and responsibility to protect everyone.

Pediatricians
It is natural for parents to avoid putting their children at risk. However, scientific research has proven the value and safety of vaccines. They save lives. Those parents who oppose them do not have accurate information about vaccines.

Concerned Parents
We know that vaccines can have benefits. However, we are also worried that they might hurt our children. We have read many stories about children having bad reactions to vaccines or developing lifelong health problems. We do not think we should be forced to put our children's health at risk.

Religious Objectors
We have a right to religious freedom. The government cannot make us to go against our religious beliefs. We have the right to control our own bodies and those of our children.

For • Supportive • Undecided • Unsupportive • Against

Disease through History

Throughout human history, people have battled diseases and developed new treatments. A great deal of progress has been made in preventing and curing many illnesses, but challenges remain.

About 400 BC

In Athens, Greece, Hippocrates writes about disease and healing. He is considered the founder of Western medicine.

AD 1347–1350

The Black Death, most likely bubonic plague, devastates Europe. More than one-third of the population dies.

1492

Christopher Columbus's first voyage begins the European conquest of the Americas. European explorers and settlers carry a wide range of diseases, including smallpox, tuberculosis, typhus, measles, and influenza. Lacking natural defenses against these diseases, millions of native peoples die.

1796

In England, Edward Jenner discovers the principle of vaccination.

1895

Nurse and social worker Lillian Wald establishes the Henry Street Settlement in New York City. It provides health care and other services to the city's poor.

1918–1919

A major influenza outbreak kills 25 million people around the world.

1928

In London, England, Alexander Fleming discovers penicillin. By the 1940s, the antibiotic becomes widely used.

1918–1919

1946

The U.S. Centers for Disease Control and Prevention is established.

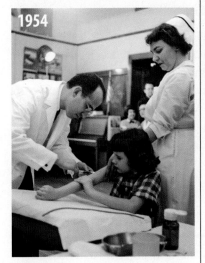

1954

1954

In the United States, widespread use begins of Jonas Salk's polio vaccine, which he first developed two years earlier.

1964

The U.S. Surgeon General's Report on Smoking and Health officially declares that cigarette smoking causes cancer and a number of other serious diseases.

1979

The last case of polio is reported in the United States.

2003

1981

The disease AIDS is identified by doctors.

2003

The Human Genome Project, an international research program, completes the task of identifying all human genes. This information is expected to help doctors treat many diseases.

2010

First Lady Michelle Obama begins the Let's Move campaign to encourage children to get regular exercise and to eat well. A goal of the program is reduce childhood obesity in the United States.

2014

Key portions of a new U.S. health-care law go into effect. They are intended to help more people in the United States obtain health insurance and access to medical care.

2010

Health Careers in Focus

EPIDEMIOLOGIST

Duties Studies the origins, causes, and spread of diseases

Education A master's degree in epidemiology, public health, or a related field

Interest Math, science, research, and problem solving

Epidemiologists are public-health specialists who study diseases. They try to understand the causes of a disease and the ways in which some illnesses spread from person to person. They play in important role in understanding epidemics and them.

Epidemiologists work in laboratories, where they analyze disease-causing bacteria or viruses. They also conduct fieldwork. Epidemiologists interview sick people and study areas in which an epidemic is occurring.

PHYSICIAN

Duties Diagnoses a patient's illness and prescribes medical treatment, as well as advises patients on how to prevent disease

Education A bachelor's degree, followed by a doctor's degree from a medical school and an internship, or training program in a hospital

Interest Biology, chemistry, and helping people

Physicians are health experts who have completed many years of training to understand and treat people's illnesses and injuries. A physician may practice general medicine or specialize in a field of treatment, such as heart disease, cancer, or surgery. Doctors also try to teach their patients about healthful living habits. During their careers, doctors must stay informed of scientific discoveries, new drugs, and other advances in medical technology.

PHARMACIST

Duties Prepares and gives out different kinds of medications

Education A bachelor's degree, often in some area of science, followed by a doctor's degree in pharmacy

Interest Public health, chemistry, medicine, and working with people

Pharmacists are experts on medications. They fill prescriptions written by doctors. This involves preparing an amount of a drug the doctor has ordered for a patient. Sometimes, pharmacists mix drugs themselves.

Pharmacists also provide drug-related information to customers. Pharmacists are responsible for pointing out safety precautions, including whether particular medicines must be taken with food. They tell the patient if a drug has side effects, such as drowsiness.

EMERGENCY MEDICAL TECHNICIAN (EMT)

Duties Responds to emergencies, provides preliminary treatment, and transports patients to a hospital

Education An EMT training program, which leads to certification

Interest Helping people, being part of a first-response team

EMTs are the first people, or responders, at the scene of an emergency medical situation. They usually arrive in an ambulance. People's lives depend on the quick thinking, actions, and abilities of EMTs. They must assess a patient's condition and provide emergency treatment as the person is being taken to a medical facility. The work is physically strenuous and can be stressful. First responders must act fast and stay calm in the face of tragedy and suffering.

Key Health Organizations

WHO

Goal Global health

Reach Worldwide

Facts WHO is a specialized agency within the United Nations

The World Health Organization (WHO) is a leading authority on global health. Headquartered in Geneva, Switzerland, it employs more than 7,000 people around the world. These people include doctors, public-health specialists, scientists, and epidemiologists. WHO also uses experts in information systems, health statistics, economics, and emergency relief.

The organization assesses the overall health of the global community. It advocates for the end of diseases and the conditions that cause them. WHO also sets international health goals, influences governmental policies, and educates the public.

CDC

Goal Protecting the health of Americans

Reach United States

Facts Distributes funds to state and local health departments, universities, and other health organizations

The Centers for Disease Control and Prevention (CDC), based in Atlanta, Georgia, focuses on health issues in the United States. It is part of the U.S. Department of Health and Human Services. The CDC views its health mission as part of protecting U.S. national security.

The CDC keeps track of the overall health of Americans. It watches out for new health threats and takes action to deal with disease-related problems. It conducts scientific research, provides health information to the public, and helps pay for research and health programs conducted by other government bodies and universities.

IFRC

Goal Crisis relief

Reach Worldwide

Facts IFRC workers include about 13 million volunteers

The International Federation of Red Cross and Red Crescent Societies (IFRC), based in Geneva, Switzerland, is a worldwide private organization that helps people in times of crisis. It is made up of national Red Cross and Red Crescent groups, including the American Red Cross. The IFRC has been working to assist people in need since 1919. It developed out of the International Committee of the Red Cross, which began in 1863.

The IFRC focuses on crisis relief in times of war or natural disaster. It provides shelter, sanitation facilities, health care, food, and drinking water to disaster victims. It also works with other organizations to make sure relief efforts are well managed.

MSF

Goal Disaster-related emergency medical care

Reach Worldwide

Facts MSF was awarded the Nobel Peace Prize in 1999

Médecins sans Frontières (MSF), or Doctors without Borders, provides emergency medical care to people suffering from natural or human-made disasters. Founded in 1971 in Paris, it is a nonprofit movement made up of 23 organizations. MSF's thousands of health professionals and support staff work in about 70 countries.

Besides helping disaster victims, MSF works to call attention to the problems of people suffering from poverty and lack of medical care. It provides information about neglected diseases. These are illnesses that cause widespread suffering but do not receive a great deal of attention from medical researchers or health-care providers.

Research a Disease-Related Issue

The Issue

Everyone agrees that good health is important and that diseases must be overcome. How to go about achieving those goals, however, can be a subject of debate. Many groups may not agree on the best ways to protect people from disease. It is important to enter into a discussion to hear all the points of view before making decisions. Discussing issues will make sure that the actions taken are beneficial for all involved.

Get the Facts

Choose an issue (Political, Cultural, Economic, or Ecological) from this book. Then, pick one of the four points of view presented in the issue spectrum. Using the book and research in the library or the Internet, find out more about the group you chose. What is important to the group? Why is it backing or opposing the particular issue? What claims or facts can it use to support its point of view? Be sure to write clear and concise supporting arguments for your group. Focus on disease causes and treatments, people's lifestyles, or relevant health laws and how your group's needs relate to them.

Use the Concept Web

A concept web is a useful research tool. Read the information and review the structure in the concept web on the next page. Use the relationships between concepts to help you understand your group's point of view.

Organize Your Research

Sort your information into organized points. Make sure your research answers clearly what impact the issue will have on your chosen group, how that impact will affect the group, and why it has chosen its specific point of view.

DISEASE CONCEPT WEB

Use this concept web to understand the network of factors contributing to disease and health.

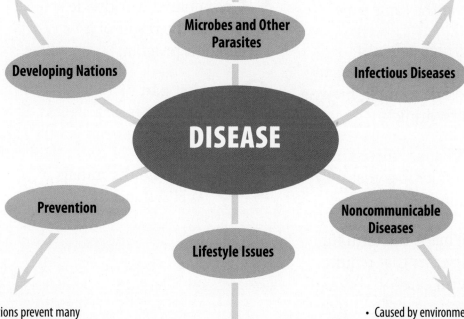

- Viruses cause illnesses from the common cold to AIDS
- Antiviral drugs often control but do not cure viral diseases
- Antibiotics can cure bacterial diseases, but "superbugs" resist antibiotics

- Children more likely to die of infectious disease than in developed countries
- Malnutrition increases the risk of disease
- Many people do not have access to clean drinking water

- Passed from one person to another through direct and indirect contact
- Carried by insects and animals
- Cause epidemics

Microbes and Other Parasites

Developing Nations

Infectious Diseases

DISEASE

Prevention

Noncommunicable Diseases

Lifestyle Issues

- Vaccinations prevent many infectious diseases
- Screening tests allow doctors to find illnesses earlier when they are easier to treat
- Access to health care is important

- Tobacco use is the greatest preventable cause of death
- Obesity may lead to diabetes, heart diseases, and other illnesses
- Lack of exercise increases a person's risk of certain diseases

- Caused by environmental, lifestyle, and genetic factors
- Include heart disease, cancer, and mental illnesses
- Responsible for most deaths worldwide

Test Your Knowledge

Answer each of the questions below to test your knowledge of diseases and health issues.

1 What disease probably caused the Black Death in 14th-century Europe?

2 What is the name for an outbreak of disease that spreads rapidly and affects a large number of people at the same time?

3 Which scientist invented a process to kill bacteria in milk, making it safer to drink?

4 What are three kinds of microbes that may cause illness?

5 What is the term for diseases that require long-term care?

6 What is a tumor?

7 What is the greatest preventable cause of death in the world?

8 What disease was eliminated worldwide in 1979 as the result of a vaccination program?

9 In what part of the body does a stroke occur?

10 What do the initials WHO stand for?

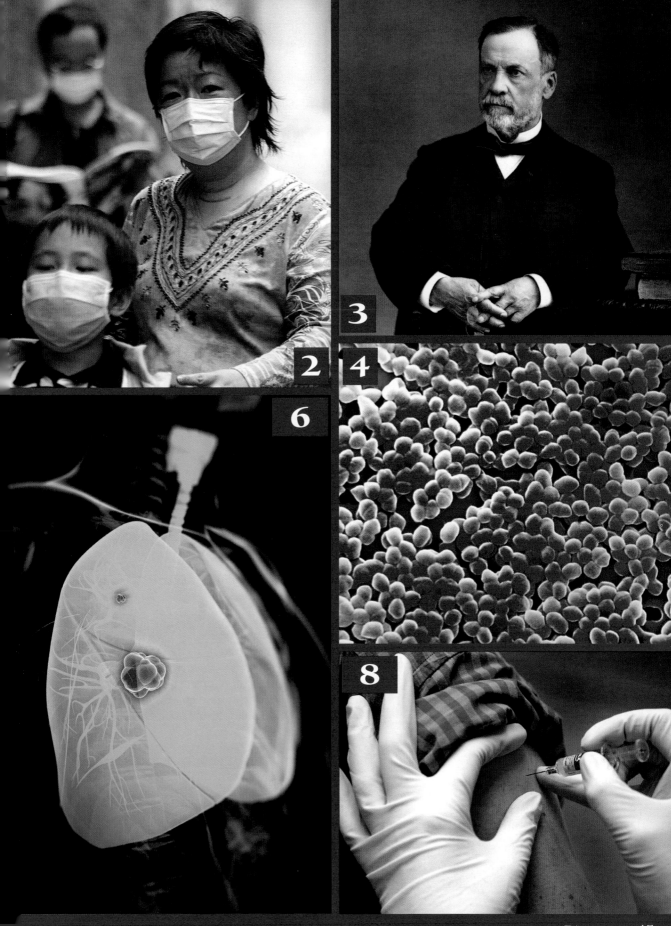

Key Words

acupuncture: a method of relieving pain or curing illness by placing needles into a person's skin at specific points on the body

alternative medicine: any of a number of healing techniques that are not used in conventional Western medicine

Alzheimer's disease: a brain disease of unknown cause that is the most common form of confusion and memory loss in elderly people

autism: a disorder affecting the brain's normal development, in which a person has language and communication difficulties

bipolar disorder: a mental disorder characterized by extreme emotional swings between activity and happiness, on the one hand, and deep depression, on the other

cells: tiny structures that make up all parts of living things

cholera: a bacterial disease of the small intestine that causes severe vomiting and diarrhea

depression: a mood disorder in which a person feels extremely sad, hopeless, and uninterested in life

developed countries: countries that have strong economies and advanced industries

developing countries: countries with low average income that until recently had little manufacturing and technology

diabetes: a condition in which people have too much sugar in their blood

diphtheria: a bacterial infection characterized by inflammation of the nose, throat, and air passages leading to the lungs

Down syndrome: a genetic disorder that causes below-average mental abilities and problems in physical development

elephantiasis: a condition, usually caused by a parasite, that causes extreme swelling

fertilized: able to grow into a new living thing

homeopathy: an alternative system of medicine that uses weakened disease-causing substances to start the body's natural system of healing

infections: illnesses caused by germs that enter the body

microbes: extremely tiny organisms, including some germs that make people sick

microscopes: devices that make tiny objects appear larger so that they can be seen more clearly

mucus: a thick liquid produced in the body that usually protects tissues

naturopathy: an alternative system of medicine that relies on diet, herbs, and exercises instead of standard drugs or surgery

organ: a part of the body that performs one or more specific functions

parasites: animals or plants that live on or in another living thing and depend on that other living thing for their survival

pneumonia: a lung disease caused by bacteria or viruses

polio: a viral disease that affects the nerves of the spine and can make a person unable to move certain muscles

schizophrenia: a serious mental illness in which someone cannot think or behave normally and has a difficult time telling the difference between reality and fantasy

smallpox: a viral disease that causes fever and a skin rash that often leaves permanent scars

strep throat: a sore throat with fever caused by a bacterial infection

tuberculosis: a bacterial disease that affects the lungs

Index

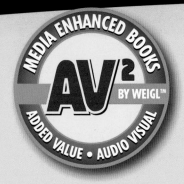

Log on to www.av2books.com

AV² by Weigl brings you media enhanced books that support active learning. Go to www.av2books.com, and enter the special code found on page 2 of this book. You will gain access to enriched and enhanced content that supplements and complements this book. Content includes video, audio, weblinks, quizzes, a slide show, and activities.

AV² Online Navigation

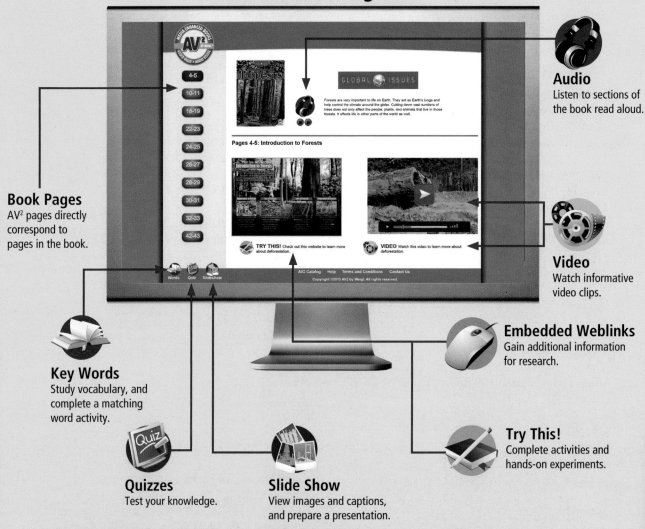

Book Pages
AV² pages directly correspond to pages in the book.

Audio
Listen to sections of the book read aloud.

Video
Watch informative video clips.

Key Words
Study vocabulary, and complete a matching word activity.

Embedded Weblinks
Gain additional information for research.

Try This!
Complete activities and hands-on experiments.

Quizzes
Test your knowledge.

Slide Show
View images and captions, and prepare a presentation.

AV² was built to bridge the gap between print and digital. We encourage you to tell us what you like and what you want to see in the future.

Sign up to be an AV² Ambassador at www.av2books.com/ambassador.

Due to the dynamic nature of the Internet, some of the URLs and activities provided as part of AV² by Weigl may have changed or ceased to exist. AV² by Weigl accepts no responsibility for any such changes. All media enhanced books are regularly monitored to update addresses and sites in a timely manner. Contact AV² by Weigl at 1-866-649-3445 or av2books@weigl.com with any questions, comments, or feedback.